Ward County Public Library
AR LEVEL 6.0
AR POINTS 0.5
AR QUIZ NUMBER 120810

21st
Century
Skills Library

ANIMAL INVADERS

ASIAN CARP

Barbara A. Somervill

Cherry Lake Publishing
Ann Arbor, Michigan

Published in the United States of America by Cherry Lake Publishing
Ann Arbor, MI
www.cherrylakepublishing.com

Content Adviser: Duane Chapman, Research Fisheries Biologist, USGS Columbia
Environmental Research Center, Columbia, Missouri

Please note: Our map is as up-to-date as possible at the time of publication.

Photo Credits: Cover and pages 1, 21, and 23, Courtesy of Chris Young/The State
Journal-Register; page 4, Courtesy of Michael Smith, Illinois Natural History Survey;
pages 6 and 15, © USDA APHIS PPQ Archive, USDA APHIS PPQ, Bugwood.org;
pages 8, 11, and 19, Courtesy of USGS; page 13, © Tony Wear, used under license from
Shutterstock, Inc.; page 17, © blickwinkel/Alamy; page 25, Courtesy of Jason Jenkins,
University of Missouri; page 26, Chicago Tribune photo by Zbigniew Bzdak; used with
permission of the Chicago Tribune

Map by XNR Productions Inc.

Library of Congress Cataloging-in-Publication Data
Somervill, Barbara A.
Asian carp / By Barbara A. Somervill.
    p. cm.—(Animal invaders)
Includes index.
ISBN-13: 978-1-60279-118-3
ISBN-10: 1-60279-118-X
1. Carp—United States—Juvenile literature. 2. Introduced fishes—United
States—Juvenile literature. I. Title. II. Series.
QL638.C94S65 2008
597'.482—dc22   2007035252

Cherry Lake Publishing would like to acknowledge the work of
The Partnership for 21st Century Skills.
Please visit www.21stcenturyskills.org *for more information.*

TABLE OF CONTENTS

CHAPTER ONE

NOT YOUR AVERAGE GOLDFISH

Asian carps jump into the air below a lock and dam in Peoria, Illinois.

When the summer heat soars, some people in Peoria, Illinois, go out on the Illinois River to take part in a new sport. It's called bow fishing. Fishers use bows and arrows to shoot Asian silver carp as they leap out of the water and over their boats. The carp are huge. Some weigh 60 pounds (27 kilograms). And they can jump 10 feet (3 meters) out of the water!

Asian silver carp are an invasive species in many rivers and lakes in the United States. An invasive species is any plant or animal that moves into—and takes over—an area where it does not naturally live.

These Asian silver carp smell like rotting bait and can be dangerous. The jumping fish have struck many water-skiers, personal watercraft operators, and boaters, causing serious cuts and broken noses and arms. They

Learning & Innovation Skills

Fishers on the Illinois River have had to deal with an oversupply of carp in the river—and not enough of the fish species they would rather be catching. Now, they are selling Asian carp in local markets. Fishers and fish sellers say that the name *Asian carp* is unappealing to buyers. Some have suggested renaming the fish to make it sound more appealing.

Do you think that it is right to change the name of the fish to try to get more people to buy it? Why or why not?

When water plants such as hydrilla take over a lake, officials in some areas have released Asian carp species to feed on the plants.

can also be destructive. Silver carp damage boats and destroy fishnets.

In Marksville, Louisiana, the future of Spring Bayou may rest in the eating habits of Asian grass carp, a close relative of the silver carp. Spring Bayou is a 2,700-acre (1,093 hectare) lake that became choked with plants such as hydrilla, water lilies, and water hyacinth. By July 2007, nearly 85 percent of the lake was completely clogged.

One answer to the excessive plant growth was to lower the lake's water level to kill some of the plant life. Another suggestion was to release Asian grass carp into Spring Bayou. Grass carp eat large quantities of water plants.

Grass carp have been used to clean up other lakes in Louisiana that have too much plant life. Officials in Marksville are considering using them for Spring Bayou. But they also know that the grass carp is an invasive species and could take over the lake in ways that won't be helpful.

CHAPTER TWO

ASIAN CARP SPECIES

Grass carp (top) and black carp are two Asian carp species that have invaded rivers and lakes in North America.

Several species of Asian carp swim the waters of the United States. They are all native to rivers in Asia. The carps most recently introduced to this part of the world are grass, bighead, silver, and black carp. Common carp is another Asian carp species. Each species has its own feeding pattern and way of life.

Common carp (*Cyprinus carpio*) are related to goldfish. But they can grow to 5 feet (1.5 m) long and weigh more than 80 pounds (37 kg)! They feed on water plants, insects, crustaceans, and dead fish. A common carp is gray-brown with a rounded snout and eyes toward the front of the head. A female lays 300,000 eggs at one time, which the male then fertilizes.

This carp species has been in U.S. waters for almost 200 years. In fact, many Americans don't realize that common carp are invaders from Asia and Eastern Europe because the fish have lived here so long. Common carp can muddy the water and uproot useful water plants, reducing other fish species. Millions of dollars are spent to control common carp in the United States.

Grass carp (*Ctenopharyngodon idella*) are often called white amur. The name *white amur* comes from the Amur River of Asia, where the species is native. Grass carp live in

eastern Asian rivers, lakes, ponds, and rice fields. Grass carp have bodies shaped like torpedoes, silvery scales, and large eyes.

These large fish can eat lots of plants each day. That is why people have introduced grass carp in some places to control unwanted plant growth. Grass carp grow quickly. They usually measure about 4 feet (1.2 m) long and weigh at least 44 to 50 pounds (20 to 23 kg).

Bighead carp (*Hypophthalmichthys nobilis*) have—guess what?—large heads! Their lower jaws stick out farther than their upper jaws. Their small eyes are set low on either side of the head. Bighead carp are native to eastern China. They spend their time near the surface of the water and feed on plankton and insect larvae.

Silver carp (*Hypophthalmichthys molitrix*) are the most-farmed fish species in the world. Farmers in the United States, however, rarely raise silver carp. This is partly because of the silver carp's excitable nature and tendency to jump, which creates problems for farmers. They are

A researcher with the U.S. Geological Survey holds up a large bighead carp. These fish can grow to be 88 pounds (40 kg)!

called filter feeders, eating mostly plankton, insect larvae, eggs, and other tiny animals.

People have introduced silver carp in some places to help control blue-green algae. This approach has had mixed results. Sometimes it has even made the problem worse.

Black carp (*Mylopharyngodon piceus*) are longer and heavier than bighead or silver carp. The biggest black carp are about 6 feet (2 m) long and 155 pounds (70 kg). They look most like grass carp, though they do not eat the same foods.

Black carp eat mollusks and crustaceans. Because black carp eat a lot of snails, farmers use them to control small parasites that attack fish in fish farms. Part of these parasites' life cycle requires a snail host. Fish farmers use black carp to eat the snails so that the parasites cannot complete their life cycle.

CHAPTER THREE

FISH INVADERS

*The U.S. government helped introduce common carp nationwide.
It turned out to have been an unfortunate activity.*

The arrival of Asian carps in U.S. waters was no accident. People brought common carp from France in 1831 as a fish for eating. Over time, different groups, including the federal government, transported and stocked fish all over the United States. Asian carps adapted so well that large numbers of them now live throughout most of the United States.

Common carp never became a popular eating fish in the United States. In fact, most people consider them pests. Common carp feed off the bottom of lakes, rivers, streams, and ponds. While down there, they stir up muck, muddying the water and killing useful plants.

Grass carp were brought from eastern Asia in 1963 to control the growth of unwanted water plants. Aquaculture operations brought in more grass carp in the early 1970s. The carp were first found in the Mississippi River in 1971. They soon showed up in the catches of commercial fishers—those who fish for a living—along the Arkansas River.

Grass carp have now invaded the waters of at least 35 U.S. states.

The range of grass carp continues to expand. In most cases, state and federal agencies, farmers, and aquaculture operations legally introduced these carp to North America. They were working to control problem plants, many of which were nonnative invaders. It was an example of one invasive species being brought in to control another!

Unfortunately, those who brought in the carps did not consider that they might grow faster and larger than native species. People did not consider that the carp might escape.

Learning & Innovation Skills

Biologists are concerned that Asian carps might affect the natural balance of America's great rivers. They worry that Asian carps are crowding out native river species such as gizzard shad and largemouth buffalo fish. Native species disappearing and invasive species flourishing could mean dramatic changes in U.S. river systems, say biologists. Possible problems may include filthy water, loss of food fish and crustaceans, and an imbalance in reservoirs and rivers.

Why should people be concerned about these problems? What, if anything, do you think can be done about them?

Three more Asian carps—bighead, silver, and black—were brought to the United States in the early 1970s. In 1972, a private fish farmer brought bighead carp to Arkansas to improve his farm's water quality and increase fish production. The fish had escaped by the early 1980s. They now live in 23 states. Fishers have even caught a few bighead carp in Lake Erie.

Black carp have not expanded their range as quickly or thoroughly as bighead and silver carp. They have slowly spread into the lower Mississippi River basin, mostly in Louisiana. In 2007, they were not considered a serious problem.

CHAPTER FOUR

ASIAN CARP PROBLEMS

An Asian carp larva swims next to its eggshell.

The biggest problem with an invasive species in water is controlling its population. Large Asian carps can lay as many as 1 million eggs a year. It is unlikely that even 1 percent of these eggs, or 10,000 eggs, will reach adulthood. But it only takes two eggs of each fish to hatch and survive to adulthood to increase the population.

As Asian carp populations exploded, they began competing with native fish species for places to feed and breed. Competition begins at the larval stage. A river can support only so many larvae and fry. The larvae feed on plankton. As the larvae become fry, they continue eating masses of food. Carp are hefty eaters, devouring large quantities of food to support their fast growth.

Bighead and silver carp adults are plankton feeders. They often feed along the water's surface. They compete directly for food with paddlefish, largemouth buffalo fish, and gizzard shad. The larvae and young of other fish species, mussels, and insects eat many of the same foods. Fishers along rivers where bighead and silver carp have become plentiful have noticed a decrease in other species that eat the same food.

Grass carp are plant eaters. They compete with crayfish, ducks, and other small plant eaters for food. They also

Researchers haul in fish from the Missouri River. This catch nets a load of bighead and silver carp and only two native fish.

eat plants that shelter the eggs of insects, frogs, toads, and other fish. Fewer nesting sites throws off the natural balance in lakes, rivers, and ponds. Loss of plants also leads to the wearing away of banks, which in turn leads to muddy waters.

Black carp feed on mollusks and snails. Many of those mollusks and snails are already critically endangered. A single black carp in the wrong place could contribute to the loss of a highly endangered mussel. Luckily, black carp have been slow to expand in the wild.

When Asian carps are introduced into an ecosystem, they can bring new diseases and parasites along with them. Often, animals native to that ecosystem have no defense against the disease or parasite. Many become sick and die.

A lake or pond is a delicate ecosystem. It includes plants and plant eaters as well as animals that hunt and animals that are hunted.

*Asian carp species outside of their natural range
have a negative effect on their ecosystems.*

Plant life provides oxygen in a pond's water and protects eggs, larvae, and young animals. But too much plant life on a pond's surface can prevent sunlight from reaching below the surface. Plant eaters provide natural gardening services. They keep water plants pruned, controlling both the amount and the variety of plants that grow.

Other species in the ecosystem—fish, snails, mollusks, and insects—need food, sunlight, oxygen, and the chance to breed. Many animal species lay their eggs on the surface of ponds, lakes, and slow-moving rivers. Some of these eggs feed a wide range of other animals. In turn, young and adult animals provide food for other, larger animals. Life moves in a cycle. And an invasive species destroys the rhythm of that cycle by reducing other species.

Why is this so important? Who cares if mussels are in the water or not? Why would anyone want pesky insects to survive? This water is what we bathe in, drink, and cook with. Nature provides us with fresh water and natural means to maintain that water. Invasive species threaten water quality because they prevent nature from keeping the water clean.

CHAPTER FIVE

STEPS TO SOLUTIONS

*Flying carp surprise this boater. Asian carps jump
when boats disturb them in the water.*

The first step in solving the Asian carp problem is research. Asian carp problems did not start overnight. And they cannot be solved quickly. It is important to learn about Asian carps in order to control their expansion in the wild.

Research has shown us that Asian carps can adapt to most freshwater environments in the United States as well as Mexico and part of Canada. Catching all of the carps is an unlikely solution. It is difficult to poison carps without poisoning their entire ecosystem. And it is surely impossible to find and get rid of millions of Asian carp eggs each year.

So what's to be done? One new option is setting up electrical fish barriers to prevent carp from moving into new waters. The U.S. Army Corps of Engineers built a temporary $2.2 million barrier on the Chicago Sanitary and Ship Canal near Romeoville, Illinois. The barrier sends electric pulses through

A U.S. Geological Survey research boat floats in front of silver carp leaping high into the air. Without solid research, any solution to the Asian carp problem is bound to fail.

the water. The electric current is not dangerous to humans, but it does startle the fish and make them turn back.

The Illinois Natural History Survey monitors carp activities near the barrier. The survey team tagged and tracked 100 common carp living in the canal. Only one tagged carp managed to pass the barrier, so work on a permanent structure began, at a cost of another $9.1 million.

A commercial fisher drives his boat full of Asian carps from the Illinois River.

Constructing electronic fish barriers is an expensive way to keep carp from advancing. But it's cheaper than the costs of doing nothing.

Another option is to remove adult fishes from the water before they can lay many eggs. Studies indicate that removing many adult bighead carp would dramatically help lower their numbers.

But what do the fishers do with the fish? They could either try to convince Americans to buy the fish, sell the fish to countries that eat bighead carp, or market it as food for animals. Scientists and business owners are working to develop various Asian carp foods and other products.

However, using commercial fishing to control the carps has some drawbacks. For example, selling Asian carps might become too profitable. Then people might spread the carp to new places in order to make more money.

A better understanding of Asian carps and their history may help control the damage they have caused. In the meantime, some states have not developed plans to control these animal invaders. When they finally do, their efforts may be too late.

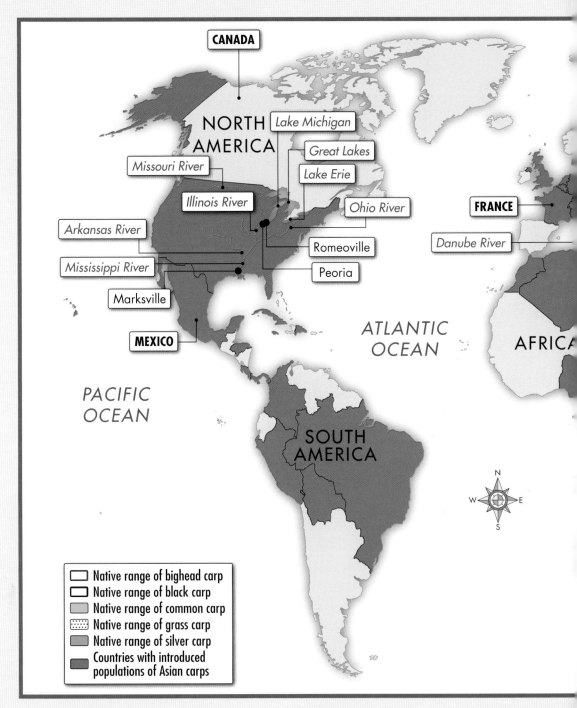

CANADA

NORTH
AMERICA

Lake Michigan

Great Lakes

Lake Erie

Missouri River

Illinois River

Ohio River

Arkansas River

Romeoville

Mississippi River

Peoria

Marksville

MEXICO

FRANCE

Danube River

ATLANTIC
OCEAN

AFRICA

PACIFIC
OCEAN

SOUTH
AMERICA

N
W   E
S

Native range of bighead carp
Native range of black carp
Native range of common carp
Native range of grass carp
Native range of silver carp
Countries with introduced
populations of Asian carps

This map shows where in the world Asian carps

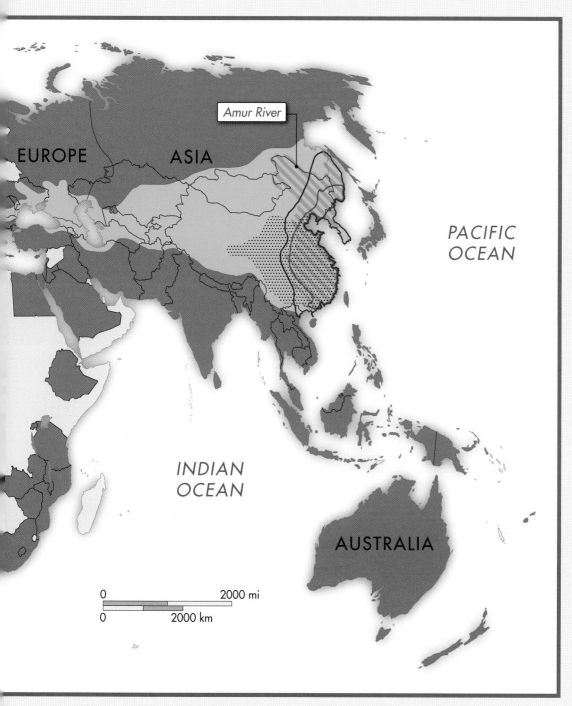

Amur River

EUROPE

ASIA

PACIFIC
OCEAN

INDIAN
OCEAN

AUSTRALIA

0   2000 mi

0   2000 km

live naturally and where they have invaded.

Glossary

algae (al-JEE) any of a group of simple living things without roots, stems, or leaves that grow mostly in water

aquaculture (AK-wuh-kuhl-chur) the business of farming fish or shrimp

conservation (kon-sur-VAY-shuhn) the preservation, management, and care of natural resources such as forests and wildlife

crustaceans (kruhss-TAY-shuhnz) animals with several pairs of jointed legs, a protective outer shell, two pairs of antennae, and eyes on the ends of stalks

ecosystem (EE-koh-siss-tuhm) a community of plants, animals, and other organisms together with their environment, working as a unit

fertilize (FUR-tuh-lize) to join male sperm with a female egg to create offspring

fry (FRY) young fish

larvae (LAR-vee) wormlike forms that hatch from the eggs of many insects

mollusks (MOL-uhsks) animals that have soft bodies, no backbone, and usually an outer shell; clams, snails, and slugs are mollusks

parasites (PEHR-uh-sites) living animals or plants that survive by feeding off, or living on or in, a host plant or animal

plankton (PLANGK-tuhn) tiny floating plants or animals that live in water; algae is plankton

species (SPEE-sheez) a group of similar plants or animals

For More Information

Books

May, Suellen. *Invasive Aquatic and Wetland Animals*. New York: Chelsea House, 2007.

Somervill, Barbara A. *Rivers, Streams, Lakes, and Ponds*. Chanhassen, MN: Tradition Publishing, 2004.

Spilsbury, Richard, and Louise Spilsbury. *The Life Cycle of Fish*. Chicago: Heinemann, 2003.

Web Sites

Asian Carp
www.wildlifedepartment.com/asiancarp.htm
To read about Asian carps and what people can do to help stop their spread

Asian Carp Management
asiancarp.org/images.asp
To see Asian carp images and learn more about these invasive species

U.S. Environmental Protection Agency—Asian Carp and the Great Lakes
www.epa.gov/glnpo/invasive/asiancarp
To learn more about how Asian carps ended up in the Great Lakes and what the U.S. Environmental Protection Agency is doing about them

INDEX

ABOUT THE AUTHOR

Barbara A. Somervill writes children's nonfiction books on a variety of topics. She is particularly interested in nature and foreign countries. Somervill believes that researching new and different topics makes writing every book an adventure. When she is not writing, Somervill is an avid reader and plays bridge.